What was it like in the past...?

Toys

Heinemann
LIBRARY

Kamini Khanduri

www.heinemann.co.uk/library
Visit our website to find out more information about Heinemann Library books.

To order:
☎ Phone 44 (0) 1865 888066
▤ Send a fax to 44 (0) 1865 314091
▭ Visit the Heinemann Bookshop at www.heinemann.co.uk/library to browse our catalogue and order online.

First published in Great Britain by Heinemann Library, Halley Court, Jordan Hill, Oxford OX2 8EJ, a division of Reed Educational and Professional Publishing Ltd. Heinemann is a registered trademark of Reed Educational & Professional Publishing Ltd.

OXFORD MELBOURNE AUCKLAND JOHANNESBURG BLANTYRE
GABORONE IBADAN PORTSMOUTH (NH) USA CHICAGO

© Reed Educational and Professional Publishing Ltd 2002
The moral right of the proprietor has been asserted.

Designed by Celia Floyd
Originated by Ambassador Litho Ltd
Printed in Hong Kong/China

ISBN 0 431 14820 1   (hardback)   ISBN 0 431 14830 9   (paperback)
07 06 05 04 03 02   07 06 05 04 03 02
10 9 8 7 6 5 4 3 2   10 9 8 7 6 5 4 3 2 1

British Library Cataloguing in Publication Data
Khanduri, Kamini
    Toys. – (What was it like in the past?)
    1. Toys – History – Juvenile literature
    I. Title
    394.2'.69146

Acknowledgements
The Publishers would like to thank the following for permission to reproduce photographs:
Bubbles: 26; Camera Press: 24; Christie's Images: 8, 12, 21; Corbis: 7; Dorling Kindersley: 19; Hulton Archive: 9, 10, 17; Museum of Childhood Edinburgh: 6, 13; Rex Features: 23; Stone: 28; Topham/ImageWorks: 29; Topham: 15, 16, 18, 20, 22, 27; TRIP/Helene Rogers: 25; Tudor Photography: 4; Victoria and Albert Museum: 5, 11

Cover photograph reproduced with permission of Hulton Archive.

Our thanks to Stuart Copeman and Noreen Marshall at Bethnal Green Museum of Childhood for their help in the preparation of this book.

Every effort has been made to contact copyright holders of any material reproduced in this book. Any omissions will be rectified in subsequent printings if notice is given to the Publisher.

Contents

Words printed in **bold letters like these** are explained in the Glossary.

Each **decade** is highlighted on a timeline at the bottom of the page.

Then and now

Playing was important to children in the past but they did not have nearly as many toys as children do today. Toy shops in the early 1900s sold toys such as trains and other toy **vehicles**, musical toys, dolls and soft toys. Many toys were made of wood or metal.

This picture shows some toys from the early 1900s.

How many different types of toys do you have? Toys are made for children to play with but adults often like them too. Some people collect old toys such as dolls or cars.

Looking at old toys can tell you a lot about the time when they were made. For example, toy trains and cars have changed over the years as changes were made to real trains and cars.

These toys were made in the 2000s. Do any of your toys look like these?

1900s and 1910s: Early toys

In the early 1900s some toys, like **hobby horses**, were made at home. Others, such as dolls, toy trains and toy soldiers, were bought in shops.

The very first teddy bear was made in 1902 in the USA. It was named after the **President** who was called Teddy Roosevelt. Teddy bears soon became popular all over the world. Do you have a teddy bear?

These teddy bears were made in Germany. Some people collect old toys like these. They can be worth a lot of money.

In the 1900s not many people had cars so horses were still an important type of **transport**. Children played with toy horses. There were large horses, small horses and even rocking horses.

During the First World War (1914–1918) when Britain was at war with Germany, fewer toys were made because many toy **factories** had to make weapons instead.

This rocking horse is made of wood and has been painted to make it look more real.

1920s and 1930s: Toy trains

Real steam trains were invented in the 1830s. The first toy trains were made soon after. These were made of wood and you pulled or pushed them along. Then **clockwork** toy trains were invented, which were made of metal.

Electric toy trains became popular in Britain in 1920. Early electric toy trains did not work very well and kept exploding.

In the 1920s, a British company called Hornby started making toy trains. This one is in its original box.

During the 1920s and 1930s toy trains were made to look like real trains. They were given the same names and colours as real trains.

You could build a train track using straight or curved pieces of rail. You could also buy tunnels, bridges, stations, signals and level crossings. All these things made up a train set or model railway.

Model railways were enjoyed by adults as well as children.

1930s and 1940s: Board games

In the 1930s and 1940s, families listened to the radio but hardly anyone had televisions. They played cards together, and board games, such as Monopoly. What board games do you play?

This little boy is playing a board game called draughts with his father.

1900 | 1910 | 1920 | 1930 | 1940

A game called Peter Rabbit's Race Game, made around 1930, is based on Beatrix Potter's book *The Tale of Peter Rabbit.*

Beatrix Potter

The Tale of Peter Rabbit was Beatrix Potter's first book. She wrote and **illustrated** 22 more books. All kinds of toys and games have been based on her stories.

In this game, players follow paths around the board and come across the sort of adventures Peter Rabbit had in the story.

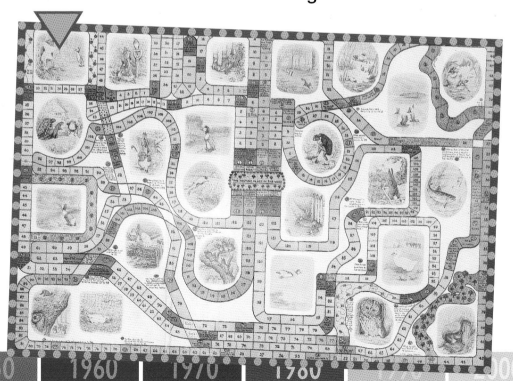

1950s: Toy cars

In the 1950s more people bought real cars. More toy cars were bought too. They were often made to look like real cars of the time.

In the 1950s Matchbox cars were very popular. Corgi cars had things like plastic windows, boots and bonnets that opened, and even working windscreen wipers.

Matchbox toy cars were so called because they were about 50mm long – just the right size to fit into a matchbox.

*Toy delivery vans often had **advertisements** painted on their sides that matched the real ones, like these for marmalade and tomato ketchup.*

All kinds of other motor **vehicles** were made too, such as trucks, tractors, delivery vans, fire engines and buses.

Collecting toy cars became a popular hobby. In some cases, a real car might only be bought by a small number of people but the toy model might be bought by millions of people.

1950s: Plastic dolls

In the 1950s dolls and other toys were made from a new type of plastic called vinyl. Vinyl was better than earlier plastics because it was strong but also quite soft, which made it easier to shape. This meant that more detail could be put into the dolls' faces, making them look more real. Do you know what your dolls are made from?

This vinyl doll was made in 1955.

1900   1910   1920   1930   1940

Queen Elizabeth II became queen in 1952 and dolls were made to celebrate the occasion. There was even a doll called Little Princess whose dress was **designed** by a man called Norman Hartnell. He was the same man who designed the dress the Queen wore for her **coronation.**

The Little Princess doll was made to celebrate the Queen's coronation.

1950s: Outdoor toys

In the 1950s, many families still could not afford televisions. Children played outside a lot with toys, such as skipping ropes and skittles.

Frisbees came from the USA. They were plastic circles with a curved edge and you sent them spinning through the air from one person to another. Do you play with the same kind of toys?

Pedal cars were popular outdoor toys.

Hula hoops also came from the USA and were very popular in the late 1950s. You stood inside the hoop, held it at waist-height, then let go and twirled your hips round and round to stop it from falling down. Have you ever tried playing with a hula hoop?

The idea was to keep the hoop spinning for as long as possible. Children spent hours practising with their hula hoops.

Hula hoops

Hula hoops are very old toys. The Ancient Egyptians played with them several thousand years ago.

1960s: Toys for building

Toys with lots of pieces that you put together to build things are called construction toys. Meccano was a metal construction toy first made in 1901 and still being made in the 1960s.

Most of the models you could build with Meccano were machines. It was made by the Hornby company which also made toy trains.

Meccano construction toys were still popular in the 1960s.

LEGO, a system of building bricks that fitted into each other, was very popular at the time. Early LEGO bricks had been made of wood but by the 1960s they were made of plastic. What kind of things do you like to build from LEGO?

In 1966, the first LEGO train went on sale. It had wheels and ran along on rails.

The meaning of LEGO

LEGO was invented by a man called Ole Kirk Christiansen. He lived in Denmark. He chose the name LEGO because the **Danish** words 'leg godt' mean 'play well'.

1960s: Dolls, trolls and robots

In the 1960s the first fashion dolls appeared. You could collect lots of different outfits for them. There was Barbie in the USA and Sindy in the UK.

The first doll for boys was called GI Joe in the USA and Action Man in the UK. People also collected trolls, which were ugly plastic dolls with long, fluffy, brightly coloured hair.

The outfits worn by Barbie often followed the fashions that people were wearing at the time.

Astronauts first landed on the moon in 1969. In the years leading up to this, there were lots of books and films about space travel and life on other planets.

Many stories had walking, talking machines called robots. Toy robots became popular too. They were usually made of metal and worked by batteries.

Toy robots walked and moved their arms and heads. Many also had flashing lights on their bodies.

1970s: TV and film toys

By the 1970s, most people had televisions and many toys were based on popular TV programmes, such as Dr Who, the Wombles and Paddington Bear. These toys often sold very well but sometimes only for a short time. They were also **advertised** on television, which helped them to sell more.

The daleks were enemy aliens in the TV series Dr Who. Dalek toys were very popular.

These action figures were based on characters in the film Star Wars.

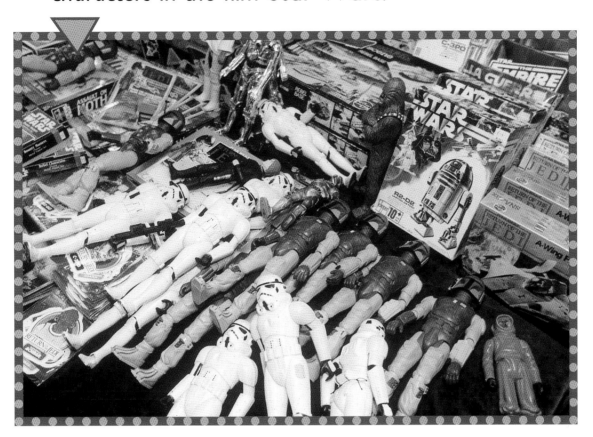

In the 1970s, the Star Wars films were made. Lots of Star Wars toys were made too, such as models of the characters in the films or of the spaceships they travelled in. Do you have any toys based on characters from films?

1980s and 1990s: Puzzles and games

The Rubik's **cube** was a puzzle invented by a Hungarian man called Erno Rubik. It went on sale in 1980.

Each side of the cube was divided into nine small squares of six different colours, all muddled up. The player had to keep twisting the squares round until each side of the cube showed nine squares that were all the same colour.

This picture shows Erno Rubik trying to solve his puzzle.

Computer games became very popular at this time. Most games were played using a television or computer screen but the Nintendo Game Boy was a hand-held computer game.

Hand-held games had their own little screens. They got their name because they were small enough to hold in your hand. Do you play computer games?

The first Nintendo Game Boy appeared in the late 1980s. The original version has been updated several times since then.

1990s and 2000s: Baby toys

Some toys are made especially for babies or very young children. Many of these, such as stacking beakers and building bricks, were first made many years ago and are still popular today. Did you play with these toys when you were little?

Black-and-white toys are good for very young babies because they can see the difference between black and white but cannot see different colours.

Television toys are popular even for very young children. At Christmas 1997, people queued all night to try and buy Teletubbies dolls.

By playing with toys, babies learn about things like shape, size and colour. They also learn about what things feel like and sound like.

Toy makers try to find ways of making baby toys safer. Young children often put things in their mouths so toys for babies are now made from materials that are safe to suck.

1990s and 2000s: Today's toys

Today, there are all kinds of electronic or computerized toys. More people now have computers at home and these are often used for playing computer games.

Many older toys are still popular. Some, such as painted wooden train sets, look much the same, but many toys have been brought up to date. Barbie dolls are still very popular and her outfits change with the times.

Computer games are popular for all ages.

1940

The Thunderbirds programmes, first shown in the 1960s, have now been shown in the 1990s. Thunderbirds toys, such as models of the spacecraft and the characters, are being sold again and are very popular.

*Yoyos were first sold in the 1920s in the USA. People liked the idea and since then, there have been regular yoyo **crazes**, the most recent being in the late 1990s.*

Find out for yourself

You can visit toy museums and look at their collections of old toys. The main one is Bethnal Green Museum of Childhood in London.

Ask your parents, grandparents or neighbours about the toys they had when they were children. Do they still have any of them?

Books

Picture the past: Toys, Jane Shuter, Heinemann Library, 1997
Toys discovered through history, Karen Bryant-Mole, A & C Black, 2001

Websites

www.bbc.co.uk/cult/retro/toys
www.batr.co.uk
www.lego.com
www.traincs.demon.co.uk

Glossary

advertise to present something to people in order to try and sell it

advertisement an announcement to sell things that can appear on television or in magazines

astronaut person who travels in space

clockwork springs and gears used to make something move

coronation when a king or queen is crowned

craze when something is popular for a short time

cube box-like shape with six equal square sides

Danish from the country of Denmark in Europe

decade ten years

design to plan something before making it, usually by drawing sketches

factory building where people use machines to make things, such as cars or toys

hobby horse toy horse often made from a broomstick and soft material for the horse's head

illustrate to explain a story with pictures

President someone who is head of a country where there isn't a king or queen

transport way of moving people or things from one place to another

vehicle a machine, often with an engine and wheels, such as a car

Index

Titles in the *What was it like in the past...?* series include:

Hardback   0 431 14826 0

Hardback   0 431 14828 7

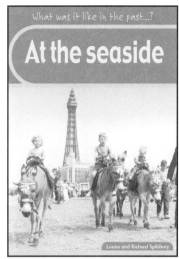

Hardback   0 431 14827 9

Hardback   0 431 14821 X

Hardback   0 431 14823 6

Hardback   0 431 14825 2

Hardback   0 431 14822 8

Hardback   0 431 14820 1

Find out about the other titles in this series on our website www.heinemann.co.uk/library